Editor

Erica N. Russikoff, M.A.

Editor in Chief

Karen J. Goldfluss, M.S. Ed.

Creative Director

Sarah M. Fournier

Cover Artist

Barb Lorseyedi

Imaging

Amanda R. Harter

Publisher

Mary D. Smith, M.S. Ed.

Authors

Peter and Sheryl Sloan

For correlations to the Common Core State Standards, see pages 78–80 of this book or visit *http://www.teachercreated.com/standards/*.

Teacher Created Resources

12621 Western Avenue

Garden Grove, CA 92841

www.teachercreated.com

ISBN: 978-1-4206-8379-0

©2016 Teacher Created Resources

Made in U.S.A.

Table of Contents

Introduction

Literacy Power was developed as a tool for teachers who are looking to support or enhance an existing reading and language-arts curriculum. The *Literacy Power* series provides teachers and students with an alternative approach to grade-appropriate material and allows teachers to reinforce reading, writing, and language skills with their students through diverse and engaging units.

Each *Literacy Power* book includes a variety of text types, such as narrative, procedural, and recount, as well as an assortment of comprehension activities inspired by the text. Each book contains a variety of high-interest topics that aim at addressing reading and writing skills in an in-depth way.

The activities in this series promote higher-level thinking and can be used to teach specific skills, reinforce information previously taught, or simply provide additional practice.

Sample activities across the series include the following:

- reading for information
- following procedures
- responding to writing prompts
- understanding details
- combining sentences
- using words in context
- determining fact or fiction
- sequencing
- interpreting pictures
- comparing and contrasting
- organizing information
- defining new vocabulary
- drawing conclusions
- matching

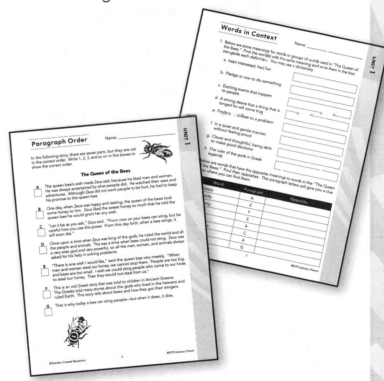

Standards

The Common Core is a set of highly researched academic standards created by teachers, school chiefs, administrators, and other educational experts. The goal of the standards is for students required to graduate high school with the same skill set and academic knowledge to succeed in future endeavors. In order for this to occur, a set of common objectives needs to be met for each grade level.

To help students become career ready, all of the texts and activities in the *Literacy Power* series have been aligned to the Common Core State Standards. To learn more about these standards, visit *http://www.corestandards.org/* or *http://www.teachercreated.com/standards/*.

The book is divided into separate units, each with a particular theme structure—either content themes or process themes. These themes are interwoven both conceptually and structurally. The content themes are based on the interests of students at their particular age and grade levels. The process themes focus on reading and writing processes.

Literacy Power provides students with a variety of opportunities to review classroom content. The activities can be used as independent or small-group practice, or they can provide teachers with opportunities for in-depth, whole-class instruction. Regardless of how you choose to use this book, the following tips may be helpful in implementing the program in your classroom.

- Introduce the workbook to your students and explain that the activities in the book will provide them with the opportunity to think about and interact with some of the concepts being taught in class, but possibly from a slightly different approach.

- Explain that the pages are designed to be easily understood. The instructions for each activity are concise and were written to be as clear as possible. Remind students to read the directions for every activity very carefully, as each activity typically requires something slightly different. Depending on the level of your students, you may want to first read the directions as a group and answer any questions.

- Allow students time to flip through the workbook to become more familiar with the layout of the pages and the various activities. Discuss any themes or activities that they seem particularly excited about or pages that pique their interest.

- Give students ample time to complete each activity, and then discuss as a class afterwards. Make note of any activities or concepts that may be more difficult and may require further review or additional instruction.

- On occasion, allow students to complete activity pages with partners. Having a discussion about the content and questions is a great way to build fluency, collaboration skills, and shared knowledge.

- *Literacy Power* was developed to focus on skills and content appropriate for a particular grade level. If you find some of your students are struggling with the content or completing the activities too quickly, consider locating a similar activity from one of the other books in the *Literacy Power* series intended for either a younger or older grade level.

Paragraph Order

Name: _____

In the following story, there are seven parts, but they are not in the correct order. Write 1, 2, 3, and so on in the boxes to show the correct order.

The Queen of the Bees

A ☐ The queen bee's wish made Zeus sad, because he liked men and women. He was always entertained by what people did. He watched their wars and adventures. Although Zeus did not want people to be hurt, he had to keep his promise to the queen bee.

B ☐ One day, when Zeus was happy and resting, the queen of the bees took some honey to him. Zeus liked the sweet honey so much that he told the queen bee he would grant her any wish.

C ☐ "Let it be as you ask," Zeus said. "From now on your bees can sting, but be careful how you use this power. From this day forth, when a bee stings, it will soon die."

D ☐ Once upon a time when Zeus was king of the gods, he ruled the world and all the people and animals. This was a time when bees could not sting. Zeus was a very wise god and very powerful, so all the men, women, and animals always asked for his help in solving problems.

E ☐ "There is one wish I would like," said the queen bee very meekly. "When men and women steal our honey, we cannot stop them. People are too big, and bees are too small. I wish we could sting people who come to our hives to steal our honey. Then they would not steal from us."

F ☐ This is an old Greek story that was told to children in Ancient Greece. The Greeks told many stories about the gods who lived in the heavens and ruled Earth. This story tells about bees and how they got their stingers.

G ☐ That is why today a bee can sting people—but when it does, it dies.

Name: _____

Understanding Details

1. Read each statement about "The Queen of the Bees." Decide if it is true (**T**), false (**F**), or no evidence (**NE**). Add the paragraph letter (**PAR LETT**) that supports your choice. The first one has been done for you.

Statement	T	F	NE	PAR LETT
a. A worker bee brought Zeus the honey.		**X**		**B**
b. Zeus could not go back on his promise because he was a god.				
c. Zeus liked honey more than any other food.				
d. The queen bee was angry because men stole honey from the beehives.				
e. The queen bee wanted to sting other bees.				
f. Zeus was entertained by people's adventures.				
g. The other gods told Zeus to be kind to women.				
h. Zeus gave the queen bee her wish.				
i. Zeus did not like men and women because they had wars.				
j. The animals, as well as men and women, went to Zeus for help because he was in the heavens and could see all things.				
k. The bees were cunning and gave Zeus a present before asking for help.				
l. The bees did not have stingers before the queen bee went to Zeus.				
m. This story is a true account of how bees got stingers.				
n. The story was told to children in Greece.				
o. Zeus let the bees sting but made it so they would die when they did because he did not like bees.				

Words in Context

Name: _____

1. Below are some meanings for words or groups of words used in "The Queen of the Bees." Find the word(s) with the same meaning and write them in the box alongside each definition. You may use a dictionary.

   a. Kept interested, had fun

   [   ]

   b. Pledge or vow to do something

   [   ]

   c. Exciting events that happen to people

   [   ]

   d. A strong desire that a thing that is longed for will come true

   [   ]

   e. Finding an answer to a problem

   [   ]

   f. In a quiet and gentle manner, without feeling proud

   [   ]

   g. Clever and thoughtful, being able to make good decisions

   [   ]

   h. The ruler of the gods in Greek legends

   [   ]

2. Below are words that have the opposite meanings to words in the "The Queen of the Bees." Find their opposites. The paragraph letters will give you a clue as to where you can find them.

Word	Paragraph	Opposite
a. happy	A	
b. boldly	E	
c. young	F	
d. start	E	
e. break	A	
f. reckless	C	
g. bored	A	
h. lives	G	

Name: _____

Sentence Combining

1. Below are some pairs of sentences. Write one sentence that has the same meaning as the two sentences in each pair.

   a. Zeus liked honey.

     The queen bee gave Zeus honey.

     _____

     _____

   b. People took the honey.

     The honey belonged to the bees.

     _____

     _____

   c. The queen bee asked Zeus to give bees stingers.

     The bees wanted to be able to sting people.

     _____

     _____

     _____

   d. Zeus gave the queen bee her wish.

     Zeus told the queen that when bees stung people, the bees would die.

     _____

     _____

     _____

   e. All the people and animals came to Zeus.

     They came because Zeus was very wise.

     _____

     _____

   f. The story about the queen of the bees gives an explanation.

     The reason has to do with why bees die when they sting.

     _____

     _____

     _____

Understanding Text

Name: _____

The Life Cycle of a Bee

Bees are insects, and like all insects, they have four stages to their life cycle.

The stages are egg, larva, pupa, and adult.

The life cycle process is called *metamorphosis*, which means that the form of the bee changes from the larva to the adult. Passing through the four stages takes 21 days for worker bees.

On the first day, the queen bee lays a single egg in each cell of the comb. Each egg generally hatches into a larva on the fourth day.

The larva is a legless grub that resembles a tiny, white sausage. The larva is fed a mixture of pollen and nectar called "beebread."

On the ninth day, the cell is capped with wax, and the larva transforms into the pupa. The pupa doesn't eat.

On day 21, a new adult worker bee emerges.

1. Write what happens during each stage of the life cycle of the bee.

   a. **1st day**

   _____

   _____

   b. **4th day**

   _____

   _____

   c. **9th day**

   _____

   _____

   d. **21st day**

   _____

   _____

Name: _____

Reading Recounts

Recounts tell about real experiences in the order in which they happened. All recounts have three parts: an **exposition**, **events** in time order, and an **ending**.

In the Waterhole

One day last summer, when the weather was hot, my three friends and I went swimming in the waterhole not far from where we lived. We had made a hut there to rest in. The waterhole is a safe place to swim and have fun.

Before we left, we packed our lunches and other gear into our backpacks. After this was done, we rode out to the hut.

When we arrived at the hut, we changed out of our clothes into our swimsuits.

As we swam around, we played games and splashed each other. We decided to have a race, and I climbed onto a log to get a diving start.

As I was about to dive off the log, it rolled away beneath me, and I fell into the water and caught my leg under the log. I could just keep my head above the water, but my leg was trapped.

When my friends heard me yelling, they came to me, but they could not lift the log off my leg. We needed help, so one of my friends stayed with me to keep my head up while the other two raced off to get help.

Soon, my friends were back at my house and telling my dad to come and get me out of the waterhole.

When my dad came, he hooked a rope around the log and pulled it away with the truck.

I had to be taken home in the truck. Perhaps the waterhole isn't as safe as I thought.

Notes

The title is in the center and is boldfaced (in this case).

The exposition tells about who, when, and where the events began.

Each event is a new paragraph.

A line is skipped between paragraphs.

This recount has seven event paragraphs.

The words that are boldfaced are time words. They tell the reader about what happened—from the first thing to the last thing. They link the recounting or telling of the story so a reader can follow more easily.

Writing a Recount

Name: _____

Writing a recount is easier if you have a plan to follow. As with all writing, the better you prepare, the better it will be. The following example shows how you can plan and write a recount.

Ideas
- (Rescue a boy)
- Whale watching
- Squashed lunch

Exposition

The Rescue
Boy fell off tree into river. Saturday, by tree. Joe, Mike, me.

Boy was thrashing in water. Nearly drowning.
Event 1

I jumped in and pulled him to the riverbank. People took him to the hospital.
Event 2

I was pleased by what I had done. The boy's parents gave me a new bike for saving his life.
Ending

The Rescue

On Saturday, Joe, Mike, and I ~~we~~ went to the river. While we were playing by the river, a boy, fell off a branch into the water. ~~the~~ (who couldn't swim)

The boy was thrashing in the water ~~he~~ because he was drowning, ~~So I jumped~~ and needed help.

I jumped in and swam out to him. I pulled him by his shirt to the river bank. Some people took him to the hospital.

I was pleased ^that I had saved him. The ^boy's parents gave me a new bike for saving his life.

The Rescue

On Saturday, Joe, Mike, and I went to the river. While we were playing by the river, a boy who couldn't swim fell out of a tree into the water.

The boy was thrashing around because he was drowning and needed help.

I jumped into the river and swam out to him. I pulled him by his shirt to the riverbank. Some people came along and took him to the hospital.

I was relieved that I had saved him. The boy's parents came to see me later and gave me a new bike for saving his life.

Note: *The final copy has some other changes to improve it that were added as it was being written. This can happen sometimes because, as you rewrite it, improvements will occasionally come to you.*

Name: _____

Writing a Recount *(cont.)*

1. Share your experiences.

   a. Make a list of three experiences you have had.

   _____

   _____

   _____

   b. After some thought, highlight the one you would like to write about the most.

   c. Think about the experience you chose. Think about the actions of people involved, what was said, colors, feelings, and so on. Write your ideas in the boxes below.

Setting	Event 1
Event 2	**Ending**

d. When completed, highlight or circle the best ideas in each box.

e. Now that you have organized what you want to write about, you are ready to write your draft. Write this draft without worrying about spelling or grammar. You are just turning your notes into sentences.

_____

_____

_____

_____

_____

_____

_____

_____

_____

_____

_____

_____

_____

_____

_____

_____

_____

_____

_____

_____

_____

Name: _____

f. When you have finished your first draft, read what you have written and edit it. Ask yourself these questions. Circle your answers.

- Does what I have written make sense?

   Yes   No

- Can I make these paragraphs better by adding adverbs, adjectives, or dialogue?

   Yes   No

- Have I used different words to replace words that I repeated?

   Yes   No

- Have I used capital letters at the beginning of my sentences and correct punctuation at the end?

   Yes   No

- Have I checked my spelling?

   Yes   No

(*Note:* Make these corrections on your draft by crossing out and adding things as shown in the example on page 11.)

2. Have a friend or the teacher read your draft and help you edit it.

3. Make any final corrections and changes that you think are needed after listening to comments made by the teacher or friends.

4. Write your final draft on a separate sheet of paper.

Recount Reminders

- Start your exposition with *when* statements; for example, "Last Saturday, my Dad went to the show." Many writers find it flows better to tell *when*, then *who*, then *where*.

- Each event in a recount is a new paragraph.

Understanding Time Words   Name: _____

Discourse markers are words in a text that give a reader a clue about how to connect the ideas in one part of a text with those in another. These words are usually found at the beginnings of paragraphs, as each paragraph is either one idea or one event. There are five kinds of discourse markers. The kind of discourse marker most often used in stories and in the telling of true experiences are the discourse markers of time.

1. Read the text.

The Fair

On Saturday, our family went to the fair. We wanted to go on the rides.

After we got our tickets, we were allowed into the fairgrounds. We walked as fast as we could to the part of the grounds where all the rides were found. We decided to go on the rollercoaster first.

When we were on the rollercoaster, we were very excited because it went really fast down the tracks and around sharp curves.

Next, we went on the bumper cars. Every car was crashing into other cars. These cars were hard to drive, but we had a lot of fun.

Soon it was lunchtime, and we went with Mom and Dad to have some food.

Later in the day, after many rides, we became very tired and went home to rest.

In the recount text "The Fair," the boldfaced words are time signals to a reader. These words do two things in this text. First, they link the paragraphs together in a specific order. Second, they tell the reader that the order of the events is set by time (going from the earliest to the latest).

The "time markers" are the main words used to start paragraphs in recount and narrative texts, because these texts tell about experiences that happen at some time.

2. Below are some of the main time markers that you will find in recounts and narratives.

before	after	now	then	while	as	soon	during
later	today	yesterday	when	since	once	next	long ago

1. In the sentences below, circle the time markers. *Note:* Not all sentences have them.

   a. Long ago, in a small town, there lived a tiny mouse.

   b. Because it was cold, the climbers stayed in their tents on the side of the mountain.

   c. When we had nearly reached the shore, we saw that the beach was covered in stones. Some of them looked like jewels sparkling in the sun.

   d. Before going to sleep, the climbers checked the tent pegs to see whether any had come loose in the wind.

   e. While the giant slept, Jack crept into the room and climbed up to the table where the hen that laid the golden eggs was sitting.

   f. If you oil the wheels on a bicycle, it will be easier to ride and go much faster.

   g. As we came sailing into the bay, we were surprised that one of the Spanish treasure ships had taken shelter there.

   h. The *Tyrannosaurus* was a large, meat-eating dinosaur.

   i. Once upon a time, there were three little pigs.

   j. Ulysses then sailed for home, weary after so many long years of war.

   k. Yesterday, a storm blew the roof off the school, so we have the day off today while the roof is being repaired.

   l. When oiling your bike, you should wipe all the dirt and grease off the frame.

   m. Captain Cook then sailed eastward into the Pacific Ocean.

   n. Long ago, in a country far away, an evil witch lived with her three black cats.

   o. Soon, we arrived at the station.

   p. After a steep climb, we reached the top of the hill.

   q. Until our journey was over, we could not rest.

Reading About Racing   Name: _____

Motor Racing

Car racing is the racing of automobiles and motorcycles. It is one of the world's most popular sports. Huge crowds of people go to see the races. There are many different kinds of car racing. Some of the most popular kinds are single-seater racing, rallying, and stock-car racing.

Single-Seater Racing

Single-seater (or open-wheel) racing is perhaps the most well known. The cars are made for high-speed racing. The wheels are not covered, and the cars have wings at the front and the rear to keep them on the track.

Single-seater races are held on special tracks or on streets that are closed for the event. Many single-seater races are held on oval tracks so that the spectators can see the whole race.

The best-known single-seater racing is Formula 1, which has very fast cars that are made to go fast for a long time.

Kart racing is a popular sport with children and adults. It is the racing of a small, low-cost machine on small tracks. Because the karts are very close to the ground, they do not have the same dangers as other kinds of motor racers. Many of today's top drivers started their careers in karts.

Rallying

Rallying, or rally racing, uses very fast cars specially set up for this sport. These cars race on (closed) public roads or off-road areas. A rally is run over different stages. The navigator helps the driver to go through each stage as fast as possible by referring to notes made while driving over the track before the race. Usually, the car with the fastest times through the stages is the winner. There are many different rallies, some of which are good for people who just like to race safely for fun.

Touring-Car or Stock-Car Racing

Stock cars are usually raced on oval dirt tracks. The cars look like those you see on the street, but they are in fact specially built race cars. Stock-car racing is very popular all around the world.

Name: _____

Caption Matching

1. After reading "Motor Racing," match the pictures below to the comments made by observers. More than one picture matches some comments.

Caption	Picture
a. "That stock car is fast. It is well ahead of the next car."	_____
b. "There goes a Formula 1 car onto the grass at the corner."	_____
c. "There are a lot of cars in this race."	_____
d. "The cars are coming around the S-bend now."	_____
e. "This stock car is racing ahead in the water."	_____
f. "The cars are bunched up at the corners."	_____
g. "The race has just started, but that car has pulled ahead of the others."	_____
h. "The Formula 1 cars corner well."	_____
i. "Number 7 is doing well for a sedan."	_____

Sentence Combining and Comprehension

Name: _____

In the space below, combine each set of sentences into one sentence. You may add or remove words, but your final sentence must have the same meaning as the set of sentences you combine. The combined sentences will make a paragraph.

Mike is the race car driver. Mike's car is a super fast stock car.

The car has alloy wheels with large, wide tires. The car has a large V8 engine to give it power.

The crowd is silent as Mike gets into his car. The people watch with interest as he starts his engine.

The engine starts with a loud roar. Mike is ready to race.

The starting flag is lowered. The race starts.

The drivers accelerate down the track. They accelerate towards the first corner.

The cars enter the corner. Two of the leading cars crash together.

Mike skillfully drives around the wrecked cars. Now he is in the lead.

Mike is running low on fuel. His engine dies as he crosses the finish line.

Mike has won the race. Mike is the new champion.

_____
_____
_____
_____
_____
_____
_____
_____
_____
_____
_____
_____
_____
_____
_____
_____
_____
_____
_____
_____
_____
_____
_____
_____

Name: _____

True, False, or Can't Tell

1. Look carefully at the picture below. Then complete the grid by checking **T** (true),
   F (false), or **CT** (can't tell) for each statement.

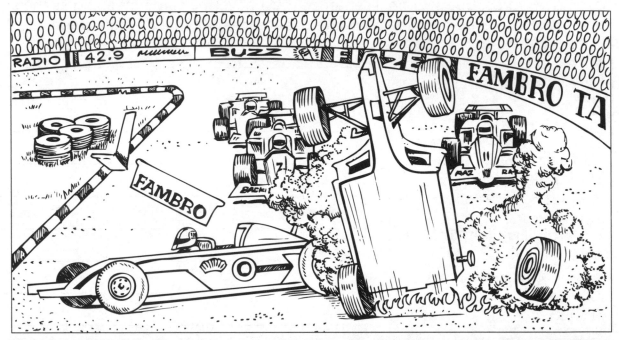

Statement	T	F	CT
a. Only one car is damaged in the crash.			
b. Many people would have seen the crash.			
c. The cars must have been going very fast.			
d. Some of the broken pieces of the crashed car are flying through the air.			
e. More than ten cars are in the race.			
f. The driver of the crashed car was taken to the hospital.			
g. A hole in the road caused the crash.			
h. An ambulance is coming out of the pit area.			
i. The accident caused a lot of damage.			
j. The car shown in the lower left is not damaged.			
k. The car flying into the air still has four wheels.			

Understanding a Text   Name: _____

1. Choose words from the list to the right to complete the sentences. The first one has been done for you.

Car racing is one of the most popular __***sporting***__ events in the world. All types of _____ are raced,
a
 but one of the biggest in terms of _____ who
b
 follow motor sports is the racing of stock cars.

Stock-car events are very exciting. The _____
c
 are very skilled, and the cars are prepared by top

_____ who can get the most out of the
d
 powerful _____.
e

Stock-car racing has many exciting moments with plenty of _____ and challenges.
f

cleaners
crashes
drivers
engines
fans
mechanics
owners
races
speeding
~~**sporting**~~
vehicles
wheels

Puzzle Reasoning

1. Here are two puzzles. Can you find the answers?

a. The first four cars to cross the finish line in a race were a red sedan, a white convertible, a blue truck, and a green SUV—but not in that order. Read the statements that follow and figure out the order of the cars as they crossed the finish line. Write your answers on the lines.

The green SUV came after the blue truck. The red sedan was second. The blue truck was not first.

1st _____   2nd _____

3rd _____   4th _____

b. Six cars were in a race. Figure out the order of the cars as they crossed the finish line.

A red convertible was ahead of the green sedan but behind the black coupe. The orange truck was between the green sedan and the white SUV. The blue van came last.

1st _____   2nd _____

3rd _____   4th _____

5th _____   6th _____

Name: _____

Paragraph Order

In the following story, there are five parts, but they are not in the correct order. Write 1, 2, 3, and so on in the boxes to show the correct order.

Why the Bat Comes Out at Night

A At the start, the birds were winning the war, so the bat joined the birds. He said that he was one of them. In one way, he was like a bird—he could fly.

B In the days before people lived on Earth, the animals and birds went to war. The bat was not sure whether he should fight for the birds or the animals. He wanted to be on the winning side.

C When he went to be with the animals, they would not have him. "No! Leave us," they said. "You only came to us because the birds would not have you. We do not want you." The bat had no one to live with, so he went off alone to live in a cave. Now the bat flies by night so that no one can see him. Even today, after all these years, neither the birds nor the animals want him with them.

D In the end, the birds won the war. The bat still wanted to be on the winners' side, so he went back to the birds.

E "No! Go away," said the birds. "You cannot join us. When we were losing the war, you left us. Go back to your animal friends."

F Then the animals won a big battle, so the bat changed sides. "I am no bird," he said. "I have no feathers. I cannot sing. It is clear that I am an animal."

Finding Evidence

Name: _____

1. Prove that the statements below are true by writing the part of the text that relates to each one.

   a. The bat was a competitive creature.

   _____

   _____

   b. The bat made use of bird-like features to persuade the birds to let him join them.

   _____

   _____

   c. The bat lives alone in a cave because no one wants to be with him.

   _____

   _____

   d. The bat was confused at first about what side of the war he should fight on.

   _____

   _____

   e. The bat is nocturnal (active during the night).

   _____

   _____

2. What do you think is the main lesson of the story?

   _____

   _____

   _____

   _____

   _____

   _____

Name: _____

Same and Different

In each row, there are two statements. In the last box of the row, write "same" if you think the statements mean the same thing or "different" if you think they mean different things.

a. The bat was uncertain on which side to fight.	The bat was unable to decide on which side to fight.	
b. The bat wanted to be on the winning side.	The bat was eager to fight so that his side would win.	
c. The bat had no one with which to live.	The bat liked to live a lonely life.	
d. The animals won a battle.	The animals won a fight.	
e. "Go back to your animal friends!"	"Go back to your animal companions!"	
f. A person who will not support his friends will soon have no friends.	No one likes a person who will not remain loyal.	
g. Achieving	Winning	
h. The bat lived in a cave.	The bat lived in a crevice in some rocks.	
i. This story is based on the fact that the bat is the only flying mammal.	This story shows that the bat is an unusual creature.	
j. All birds have feathers. The bat has no feathers, so it is not a bird.	Most birds fly. Bats can fly, so they must be birds.	

24

Report Text Structure

Name: _____

We often talk about groups of things that have the same or similar looks, live in the same places, and do the same actions. Study the report below. It has four paragraphs. Each paragraph gives the reader a different type of information.

Information Type	Report
	The Bat
Classification (what it is)	The bat belongs to the animal class *mammalia*. It is the only flying mammal.
Description (what it has or looks like)	The bat has a small body. It has skin that joins its front limbs and body so that when it stretches its arms, it has wings.
Location (where it is found and lives)	The bat lives in caves, trees, or dark places.
Dynamics (what it does and how it acts)	The bat can fly well. The bat eats mostly insects.

Look at the report above and complete the sentences below to help you learn and remember how reports are structured. A report is a type of writing (text) that organizes information in a scientific way. A true report has four kinds of paragraphs: classification, description, location, and dynamics.

1. Complete these sentence starters.

    a. A report is a _____

    _____

    b. The classification paragraph _____

    _____

    c. The description paragraph _____

    _____

    d. The location paragraph _____

    _____

    e. The dynamics paragraph _____

    _____

Name: _____

Meaning Grid (Reports)

1. Read each statement. Decide where it belongs in a report by placing an ✗ in the correct column.

	Classification	Description	Location	Dynamics
a. The eagle is a bird.				
b. The elephant has a large body with thick legs.				
c. Lions are good hunters that eat other animals.				
d. The wombat lives in a burrow.				
e. A snake is a reptile.				
f. The polar bear has thick, white fur on its body.				
g. Dolphins are fast swimmers.				
h. *Tyrannosaurus* was a dinosaur.				
i. Termites live in nests.				
j. The tiger has strong teeth.				
k. The kangaroo can hop.				
l. Mice have long tails.				
m. A canine is a mammal.				
n. The elephant has one calf.				
o. The grey wolf hunts in packs.				
p. Moose live near lakes and rivers.				
q. The chipmunk lives in North America.				
r. The llama is a member of the camel family of animals.				

Paragraph Order

Name: _____

In the following text, the last five paragraphs (A–E) are not in the correct order. Write numbers in the boxes (4–8) to show the correct order.

Battle of the Giants

Tyrannosaurus was one of the largest meat-eating dinosaurs. With huge, powerful jaws, it was also one of the fiercest. The teeth of this great beast were up to 12 inches long and very strong and sharp. *Tyrannosaurus* had big, strong rear legs with tough, sharp claws. With those powerful jaws, sharp teeth, and strong rear legs, *Tyrannosaurus* could rip flesh and easily kill other animals.

Plant-eating dinosaurs had beaks for chewing plants, but they did not have sharp teeth to defend themselves. Many plant-eaters, however, were protected by thick plates of bone that covered their bodies. Some plant-eaters, such as *Triceratops*, also had large horns that could rip the flesh off their enemies. Most plant-eaters could run much faster than the large meat-eating dinosaurs.

Ankylosaurus was a huge plant-eater. It was as big as a large army tank. Its body was covered with hard bony plates. The tail was long and heavy, studded with spikes, and had a large "club" (made of bone) at the end.

A ☐ The fight lasted a short while as each dinosaur pulled at the other. As they fought, their huge footprints were left in the thick, muddy ground.

B ☐ Millions of years after this great battle, the skeleton of the *Tyrannosaurus* was found alongside its own footprints and the footprints of the *Ankylosaurus* that got away.

C ☐ Once, millions of years ago, a *Tyrannosaurus* roamed near a lake. It was hungry, so it stalked a herd of ankylosaurids.

D ☐ *Tyrannosaurus* hid among trees. When an *Ankylosaurus* came near, the *Tyrannosaurus* sprang out and tried to close its jaws over the *Anklosaurus*'s neck, but the neck was too thick and hard.

E ☐ Suddenly, the *Ankylosaurus*, who was a very strong beast, swung its heavy, clubbed tail. The large bone "ball" on the end of the tail smashed into the leg of the *Tyrannosaurus* and broke it. The *Tyrannosaurus* could not stand on one leg, and so it crashed to the ground where it was eaten by other meat-eaters.

Name: _____

Fact or Opinion

1. Read each statement and decide if it is a fact or an opinion by rereading "Battle of the Giants." Write your choices in the boxes.

Statement	Fact or Opinion
a. *Tyrannosaurus* was not the largest dinosaur.	
b. *Tyrannosaurus* was the fiercest dinosaur.	
c. Some plant-eaters had large horns.	
d. *Ankylosaurus* would have been better than *Triceratops* at protecting itself.	
e. The tail of the *Ankylosaurus* was used for defense.	
f. Most plant-eating dinosaurs were faster than meat-eating dinosaurs at running.	
g. Perhaps the end of the dinosaurs came when there were no more plant-eaters left alive to feed the meat-eaters.	
h. *Ankylosaurus* was the most intelligent plant-eating dinosaur.	
i. *Ankylosaurus* was the best plant-eater at fighting.	

28

Finding Facts

Name: _____

Read the facts about dinosaurs.

Stegosaurus—plant-eater

Length: up to 30 feet long

Height: up to 14 feet tall

Weight: up to 7,000 pounds

Late Jurassic period

156–140 million years ago

Carcharodontosaurus— meat-eater

Length: up to 44 feet long

Height: up to 12 feet tall at the hips

Weight: up to 16,000 pounds

Middle Cretaceous period

110–90 million years ago

Triceratops—plant-eater

Length: up to 27 feet long

Height: about 10 feet tall

Weight: up to 26,000 pounds

Late Cretaceous period

72–65 million years ago

Brachiosaurus—plant-eater

Length: up to 85 feet long

Height: 40–50 feet tall

Weight: up to 120,000 pounds

Late Jurassic period

156–145 million years ago

Tyrannosaurus—meat-eater

Length: up to 40 feet long

Height: up to 20 feet tall

Weight: up to 14,000 pounds

Teeth: up to 12 inches long

Late Cretaceous period

85–65 million years ago

Allosaurus—meat-eater

Length: up to 38 feet long

Height: up to 17 feet tall

Weight: about 6,000 pounds

Late Jurassic period

150–140 million years ago

Ankylosaurus—plant-eater

Length: up to 35 feet long

Height: up to 4 feet tall

Weight: up to 8,000 pounds

Late Cretaceous period

70–65 million years ago

Name: _____

Comparing and Contrasting

1. After carefully reading "Finding Facts," complete the questions below. You will need to formulate some answers by analyzing the pictures and their fact boxes.

a. List the plant-eating dinosaurs in order of weight, heaviest to lightest.

_____

_____

_____

b. Why couldn't *Tyrannosaurus* kill *Brachiosaurus*?

_____

_____

_____

c. List the dinosaurs by their height, tallest to shortest.

_____

_____

_____

_____

d. List two dinosaurs that would have been possible food for *Tyrannosaurus*.

_____

_____

e. Give one possible reason why *Allosaurus* and *Tyrannosaurus* did not have armor plates.

_____

_____

_____

f. *Brachiosaurus* had no sharp teeth or claws and no armor. How did it defend itself?

_____

_____

_____

g. List the dinosaurs by their length, longest to shortest.

_____

_____

_____

_____

h. What living animal today would you compare to *Triceratops*?

_____

i. List three differences between *Tyrannosaurus* and *Allosaurus*.

_____

_____

_____

_____

j. Fill in the missing time frames for each of these periods.

Late Jurassic

_____ to _____ million years ago

Middle Cretaceous

_____ to _____ million years ago

Late Cretaceous

_____ to _____ million years ago

Name: _____

Graphic Organizer

Below is an example of facts about a dinosaur sorted into a graphic organizer that makes it easier to write them into a report. Look at it carefully.

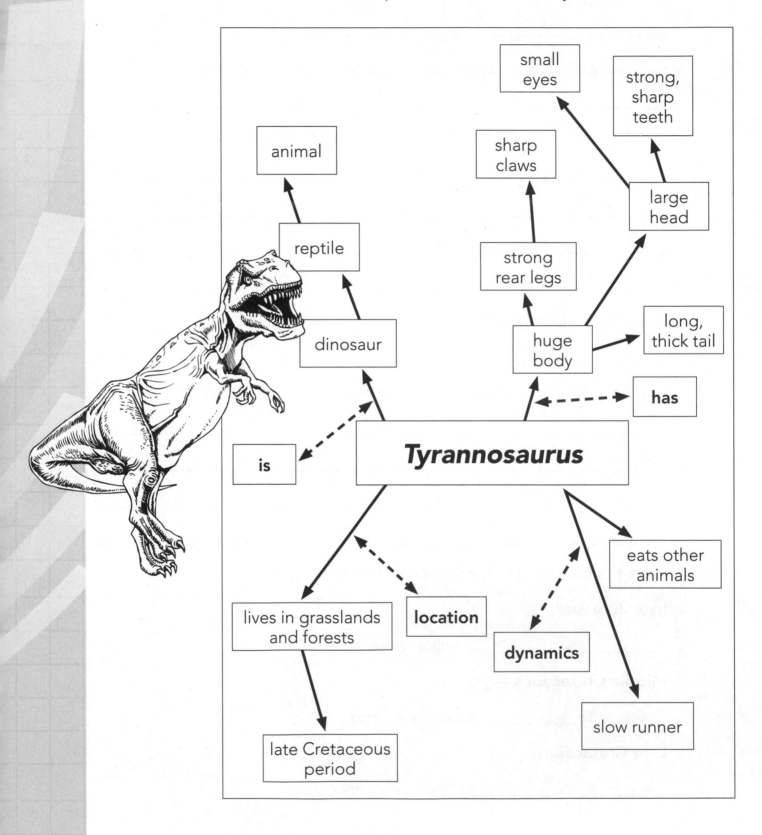

Organizing Facts

Name: _____

1. Write facts about the crocodile in the graphic organizer below. The facts are below the graphic organizer. One fact will go in each box.

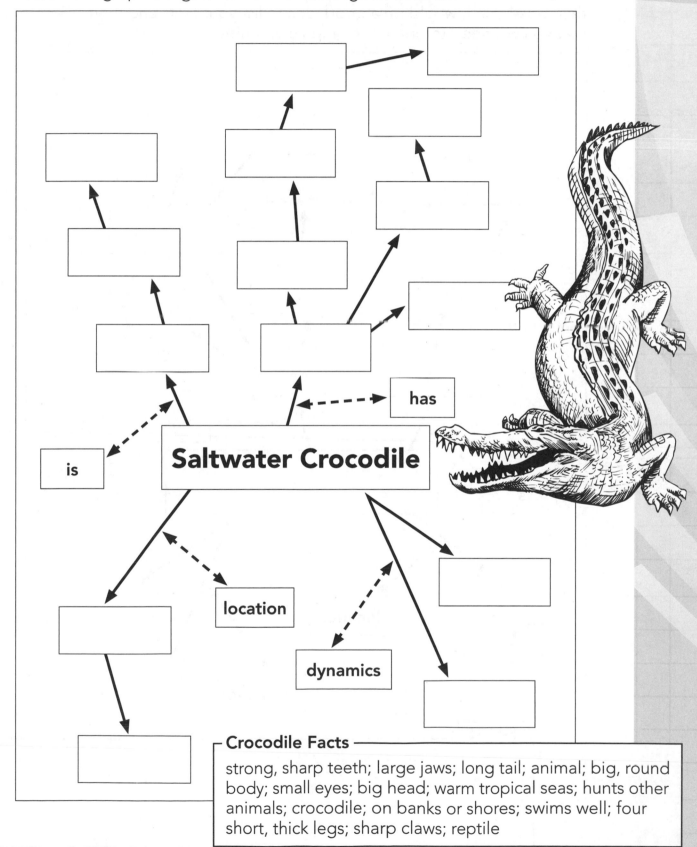

Saltwater Crocodile

is

has

location

dynamics

Crocodile Facts

strong, sharp teeth; large jaws; long tail; animal; big, round body; small eyes; big head; warm tropical seas; hunts other animals; crocodile; on banks or shores; swims well; four short, thick legs; sharp claws; reptile

Organizing Facts *(cont.)*

UNIT 6

2. Below is a graphic organizer for facts about an animal of your choice. You may need to research the facts from a book or the Internet. You may have more facts than boxes, so it would be a good idea to list your facts and then select those that you will need to put in the graphic organizer.

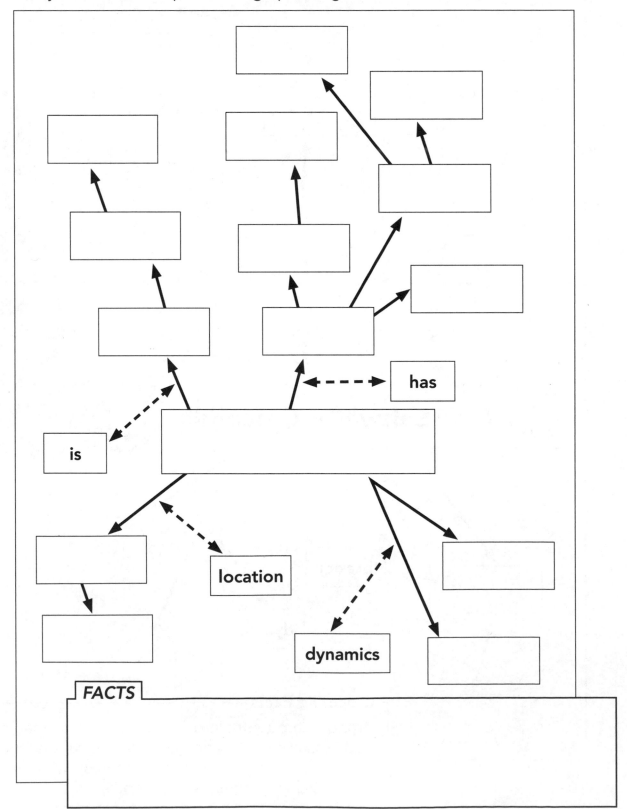

About Reports

Name: _____

The *Tyrannosaurus* reports in the boxes below show how a graphic organizer (see page 32) may be used to write a report. The first report is short, using only a few facts. The second report is longer, using all the facts from the *Tyrannosaurus* graphic organizer. These examples will help you write reports of your own. (*Note:* The **X**s show where there is a line break between the paragraphs.)

Title	***Tyrannosaurus***
	X
Classification	*Tyrannosaurus* was a dinosaur.
	X
Description	*Tyrannosaurus* had a large body and head.
	X
Location	*Tyrannosaurus* lived in forests and grasslands.
	X
Dynamics	*Tyrannosaurus* ate other animals.

Title	***Tyrannosaurus***
	X
Classification (what the animal is)	*Tyrannosaurus* was a dinosaur. A dinosaur belongs to the reptile group of animals.
	X
Description (what the animal has or looks like)	*Tyrannosaurus* had a huge body with large, strong rear legs that had sharp claws. It had a long, heavy tail. The head of this dinosaur was large, with small eyes and long, very sharp teeth.
	X
Location (where the animal is found or lives)	*Tyrannosaurus* lived in the forests and grasslands. It was alive during the late Cretaceous period.
	X
Dynamics (what the animal does and how it acts)	*Tyrannosaurus* was a fierce hunter. It ate other animals.

Name: _____

Writing a Report

Using the graphic organizer you completed on page 34, write a report. Use some or all of the facts from your graphic organizer. The skill of writing good reports is to keep the facts that belong together in the same paragraph. Your report does not need to be long, but it must have four paragraphs, as in the examples on the previous page.

To guide you, the framework of the report is shown on the left. Remember to skip a line between paragraphs and after the title. If necessary, finish your report on a separate sheet of paper.

Title

Classification (what the animal is)

Description (what the animal has or looks like)

Location (where the animal is found or lives)

Dynamics (what the animal does and how it acts)

Check Your Work

1. Does what I wrote make sense?

2. Did I spell everything correctly?

3. Did I use the correct punctuation?

Reading for Information

Name: _____

Read the following text, keeping this question in mind as you read:

> **Could monster animals be living, hidden away, and unknown to people?**

Living Monsters

All over the world, people tell of experiences in which they have seen large beasts. Many scientists say that the beasts do not exist and that the stories are made up, or that the people who saw these beasts just saw ordinary animals or some other object and imagined that they saw a monster.

Although scientists have yet to capture any of these monsters and examine them, the fact is that there are hundreds of these stories from all areas of the world. The recounts are very much alike. The monsters have been seen at many different times and places.

Many very important and trustworthy people have seen monsters. Sea captains, explorers, doctors, and others have all seen monsters. Perhaps these people are telling lies, but it is unlikely. In a lot of accounts, the monsters were seen by more than one person at one time. On a few occasions, villagers living in remote places are said to have been attacked by the monsters.

The Loch Ness Monster

Loch Ness is a remote Scottish lake surrounded by high mountains. The waters are dark and very cold. Until 1933, not many people had ever seen the lake, and so the reports of a lake monster were not taken seriously. In 1933, a road was built along the side of the lake, and thousands of people began to travel on the road. In May of that year, Mr. John Mackay was driving along the road when he saw something large in the water. He stopped to look. He saw a huge thing that looked like the back of a whale rise up out of the water.

In the next few months, many people traveling on the road reported seeing the "monster," as newspapers called it. Some took photographs. Some of the people who had a better view said that the monster had a very long neck with a small head. In 1934, Mr. Wilson took a photograph that seemed to show a long neck and small head sticking up out of the lake, with a large body beneath the surface.

Living Monsters (cont.)

In the 1960s, people became interested in the beast when Tim Dinsdale filmed it. The Lowrie family were sailing in their boat on the lake when they saw a large thing following them. It had a huge body and a long neck. The Lowries sailed away as fast as they could.

In 1969, a boat with a sonar (an instrument that sends out beeps of sound and measures them when they bounce back) picked up a large object about 500 feet beneath the surface. In 1972, a team of scientists explored the lake with sonar and underwater cameras. They found many large objects deep in the lake and took three very interesting photos that seemed to show a large animal.

Meanwhile, more and more people reported seeing the large beast. It seems that the monster is between 20 and 30 feet long with a long neck, small head, huge round body, and flippers.

From the descriptions, the monster sounds like a large reptile called the *Plesiosaurus*. Some people believe that these reptiles were trapped in the lake when it was cut off from the sea as the land rose after the last ice age.

Loch Ness is not the only lake where monsters have been seen. In Northern Ireland, Canada, and Africa, large monsters have been seen in lakes. In all the lakes where monsters have been seen, there are large numbers of fish for big beasts to eat, so it is not impossible that animals from the dinosaur age could have survived in their dark, murky waters.

Although no one has captured a monster from Loch Ness, reports of sightings continue to happen frequently. "Nessie," as the beast has been called, continues to excite visitors and has become famous worldwide.

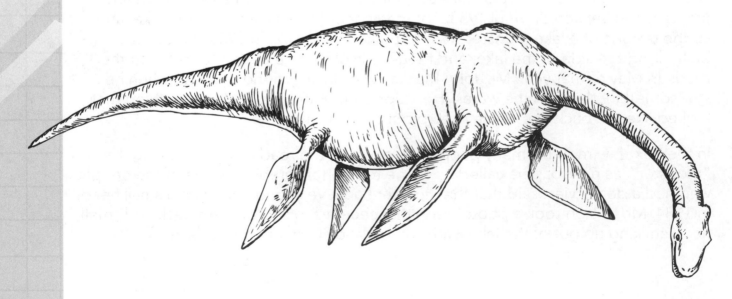

Event Order

Name: _____

1. Write a number in the box alongside each statement from the text to show the correct order of the "Living Monsters" text. The first number and last number have been written for you.

   a. Sonar located a large object 500 feet down in the lake. ☐

   b. Loch Ness was not seen by many people until 1933. ☐

   c. "Nessie" may be a *Plesiosaurus*. ☐

   d. Despite the many sightings, scientists have not yet captured one of these monsters. ☐

   e. "Nessie" is the most famous monster. **15**

   f. Monsters have been seen by many people at one time. ☐

   g. John Mackay sees a large object in the lake. ☐

   h. Dinsdale films "Nessie." ☐

   i. A team of scientists finds many large animal-like objects in the lake. ☐

   j. A family on a boat is chased by a monster. ☐

   k. From reports, the monster is up to 30 feet long. ☐

   l. Many scientists say these monsters do not exist. **1**

   m. In 1934, Mr. Wilson takes a photograph. ☐

   n. Other lakes throughout the world have large creatures in them. ☐

   o. Many road travelers see the monster. ☐

Name: _____

Evaluating Details

1. There are six areas of information in the following outline. Each section contains four statements that are either factual and sensible or not factual and not sensible. Compare these statements with information from the "Living Monsters" text, marking a check next to those that are supported by the text.

   a. **The number of reports about monster beasts**

   ☐ Reports about large beasts have been made in Scotland.

   ☐ Reports about large beasts are very widespread.

   ☐ Reports of monster beasts have been received from many countries.

   ☐ Reports have not been made in the last 100 years.

   b. **Scientists' opinions**

   ☐ All scientists say these large animals do not exist.

   ☐ Many scientists believe that people have only imagined these beasts.

   ☐ Many scientists believe that people have only seen ordinary animals.

   ☐ Some scientists think that the beasts do exist.

   c. **Who claim to have seen a monster?**

   ☐ Sea captains claim to have seen large monsters.

   ☐ Doctors claim to have seen monsters.

   ☐ Only untrustworthy people claim to have seen large beasts.

   ☐ People who claim to have seen large beasts are always lying.

Evaluating Details (cont.) Name: _____

d. **Various reports**

☐ Prior to 1933, Loch Ness was not seen by people.

☐ Visitors to Loch Ness increased greatly after 1933.

☐ Many people traveling on the road built along Loch Ness in 1933 claimed to have seen the monster.

☐ A movie taken of the monster in the 1960s greatly increased interest in the monster.

e. **What is "Nessie"?**

☐ Nessie may be a surviving reptile called a *Plesiosaurus*.

☐ It is 50 to 60 feet long.

☐ It has a very long neck with a large, round body and flippers.

☐ Sonar searches show large animal-like objects in the lake.

f. **Is there proof that "Nessie" exists?**

☐ Loch Ness is the only lake where monsters are said to live.

☐ Nessie lives in a Canadian lake.

☐ It is possible for some dinosaurs to have survived in the deep waters of Loch Ness.

☐ There are no fish in Loch Ness, so Nessie could not live there.

Name: _____

Imaginative Report

Below is an example of an imaginative report. It is exactly like a real report in the way it is written, except that the information is imagined. Read it carefully.

The Elekang

The elekang is a mammal. It is a cross between a kangaroo and an elephant.

Elekangs are huge beasts with big bodies and legs like tree trunks. They have long tails, large ears and eyes, and sharp tusks. Their bodies are covered in gray fur. Underneath are large pouches, big enough to carry small cars.

Elekangs live in towns as well as in the Australian Outback. They make a home wherever they like. A house will only last a week before it is crushed as they move around.

This friendly beast likes to dance and play a game called "throwing cars" with its huge trunk. Elekangs eat about four tons of ice cream a day. When they jump, they leave huge holes in the ground.

Title

The first paragraph classifies the animal. It tells what it is.

A line is skipped between paragraphs.

The second paragraph tells what the animal has and what it looks like, like its size, shape, and color, as well as important body features.

The third paragraph tells where the animal is found and where it lives, as well as facts about its habitat.

The fourth paragraph tells what the animal does.

Writing an Imaginative Report

Name: _____

Write an imaginative report using the example on page 42 as a guide. Follow the guidelines on the left.

Title

Each paragraph starts at the margin.

A line is skipped between paragraphs.

The first paragraph classifies the animal. It tells what it is.

The second paragraph tells what the animal has and what it looks like, like its size, shape, and color, as well as important body features.

The third paragraph tells where the animal is found and where it lives, as well as facts about its habitat.

The fourth paragraph tells what the animal does.

Name: _____

Paragraph Order

In the following story, there are five parts, but they are not in the correct order. Write 1, 2, 3, 4, or 5 in the boxes to show the correct order.

The Lazy Sons

A ☐ After a while, he had an idea. He gathered his sons together. "I must tell you this secret in case I am soon gone," he said. "There is a large treasure on this farm. You will find it buried in the fields."

B ☐ That year there was a great harvest, and the brothers had to work hard to get the crops in and sell them. The boys made a lot of money from their crops.

C ☐ The boys talked about what they had done. They saw what their father had meant. There was a treasure in the fields, but it did not come from buried treasure; it came from hard work.

D ☐ The lazy boys liked money. They set out to find the treasure. The oldest son dug up the north field. The second boy dug up the south field. The third boy took the west field. The youngest son searched the east field. They dug and they dug, but they found nothing. "Now that the fields are all dug up, we might as well plant crops," said the sons. So they did.

E ☐ A farmer was worried. He had four big, strong sons. The boys were lazy. They never worked. "What will happen when I am gone?" the farmer said. "The farm will become a wasteland. The lazy boys will not plant, and they will grow no crops."

Wrong to Right

1. Below are some incorrect statements made about "The Lazy Sons." Rewrite the statements so that they are correct.

   a. There was a carpenter who had five small and weak sons.

   _____

   _____

   _____

b. The carpenter's sons liked to work hard, and so they worked all the time.

_____

_____

_____

c. The mother had an idea, so she called her daughters together.

_____

_____

_____

d. The farmer told his sons, "There is food hidden on the farm. You will find it hidden in the trees."

_____

_____

_____

e. The sons liked food, so they searched through the trees. One son chopped down the east forest, another the west forest. The third son hacked down the south trees, and the last two sons chopped up the north forest.

_____

_____

_____

Name: _____

Choose the Sentence Ending

1. Choose the correct ending to each sentence starter by checking the correct box.

a. **"When I am gone" means the farmer**

☐ would be gone far away in another country.

☐ was leaving home for some time and would not be able to be contacted.

☐ would be deceased.

☐ needed money.

b. **The farmer worried about what would happen when he was gone because his sons**

☐ did not like to plant crops.

☐ were not farmers.

☐ did not like to get money from the farm.

☐ were lazy and would not work together.

c. **The farmer's idea shows that the farmer**

☐ was a man who had secrets.

☐ was a rich man with a buried treasure.

☐ could not remember where the treasure was hidden and so he wanted his sons to find it.

☐ was a cunning man who tricked his sons into doing work.

d. **This story teaches**

☐ that treasures are often found in fields.

☐ that laziness will never make anyone rich.

☐ that hard work is a treasure.

☐ that by working hard, money can be made more certainly than by digging for a treasure.

Fact or Opinion

Name: _____

1. Check the box alongside each statement to show whether it is a fact or an opinion. When applicable, write the paragraph letter from "The Lazy Sons" that supports your choice.

Statement	Fact	Opinion	Evidence: Paragraph Letter
a. The sons were eager to get money.			
b. The farm had four fields.			
c. The farm would be a wasteland when the farmer was gone.			
d. It took the sons quite a long time to dig all the fields.			
e. The farmer was a rich man.			
f. The farmer had no cows or sheep, only crops on the farm.			
g. Although lazy, the sons were smart.			
h. The farmer had died before the sons planted the next crop.			
i. The fields were all about the same size.			
j. The crops the sons planted made a lot of money.			
k. The sons were never lazy again.			
l. The sons planted more crops the following year.			

Name: _____

Combining Sentences

1. Below are some groups of sentences. Write one sentence that has the same meaning as the sentences in each group.

    a. A farmer was worried.

       The sons were very lazy.

       The sons did no work.

    _____

    _____

    _____

    b. The farmer told his sons.

       He told the sons that there was treasure.

       The treasure was buried in the fields.

    _____

    _____

    _____

    c. The sons loved money.

       The sons dug up the fields.

    _____

    _____

    d. The sons found no treasure.

       They planted seeds in the ground they had dug.

    _____

    _____

    e. The seeds grew into a large crop.

       The crop was a good crop.

    _____

    _____

Picture Interpretation   Name: _____

1. Look carefully at this picture and complete the following activities.

2. Read each statement. Decide if it is true (**T** = the picture shows the statement is true), false (**F** = the picture shows that it is false), probably true (**PT** = you think it is probably true), or probably false (**PF** = you think that it is probably false).

Statement	T	F	PT	PF
a. The man hanging from the tree is the driver of the car at the bottom of the cliff.	☐	☐	☐	☐
b. There are five men holding the safety net.	☐	☐	☐	☐

Statement	T	F	PT	PF
c. A helicopter is coming to help rescue the driver.	☐	☐	☐	☐
d. The driver of the crashed car is a woman.	☐	☐	☐	☐
e. The car on the rocks is not badly damaged.	☐	☐	☐	☐
f. The man on the bend of the road is waving flags at the helicopter pilot.	☐	☐	☐	☐
g. A man in the helicopter is skilled at rescuing people.	☐	☐	☐	☐
h. An ambulance is waiting to take the driver to a hospital.	☐	☐	☐	☐
i. A climber is bringing a rope up the cliff face.	☐	☐	☐	☐
j. A man is climbing down the rope to grab the driver.	☐	☐	☐	☐
k. The hanging driver is not worried about hanging from the tree.	☐	☐	☐	☐
l. The cliff is too high to jump from.	☐	☐	☐	☐

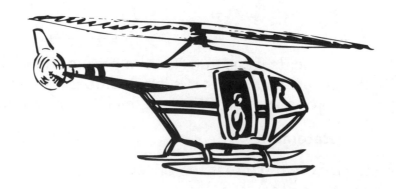

Reading Procedures

Name: _____

Read the text below. It is a procedure. Procedure texts tell how something is done.

How to Make a Jet Balloon

Goal

The jet balloon is an easy toy to make. The instructions below explain how some students made one. This toy is a good example of how we use energy. After reading this procedure, you will know how to make your own jet balloon.

Materials

First of all, the students found all the materials they needed to make the jet balloon.

- a ball of thin string

- a few balloons

- a plastic drinking straw

- a pair of scissors

- some sticky tape

Method (Steps for Making a Jet Balloon)

1. First, the students unwound the ball of string and tied one end to a doorknob in a large room.

2. Next, the students stood at the other side of the room and pulled the string tight. The string was then cut.

3. After this, the students used the scissors to cut about 2 inches off the plastic straw.

4. The students then blew up the balloon and held the neck so that air could not escape. The energy the students used to blow up the balloon is now in the balloon in the form of compressed air.

5. Then some strips of sticky tape were cut and used to stick the small piece of the straw onto the balloon.

6. Following this, the students threaded the end of the string through the straw and pulled the string tight.

7. The balloon jet was now made and ready.

How to Make a Jet Balloon *(cont.)*

Trying Out the Procedure

The students then let the balloon go, and the balloon flew across the room on the string.

By trying bigger balloons and balloons of different shapes, the students were able to make some jet balloons that would travel a long way.

How the Jet Balloon Works

The jet balloon gets its energy from the compressed air inside it. The person who blew up the balloon has put energy into it in the form of compressed air.

When the air under pressure is released, it rushes out the end of the balloon and pushes the balloon in the opposite direction.

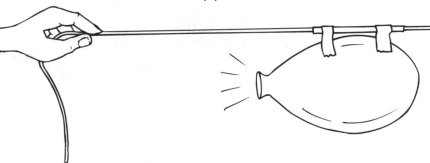

Drawing Conclusions

1. To answer the question below, you will need to think of reasons why certain materials were chosen and how they were used in the procedure for making a jet balloon.

   a. Why does the tape used have to be sticky?

   _____

   _____

   _____

Drawing Conclusions *(cont.)*   Name: _____

   b. Why is a piece of drinking straw a good way of attaching the balloon to the string?

_____

_____

_____

   c. Give reasons why a larger balloon might go faster and farther than a small balloon. How would you prove it?

_____

_____

_____

   d. Why is the tightness of the string an important factor in how well the balloon jets along?

_____

_____

_____

_____

   e. Why would you use only a small section of the plastic straw?

_____

_____

_____

   f. Think of one other way this idea of air escaping under pressure might be used. Describe it on the lines below.

_____

_____

_____

Name: _____

Identifying Procedure Texts

From your reading of "How to Make a Jet Balloon," you will know that a procedure tells how to do something. It tells a reader four types of information:

- What the **goal** of the procedure is

- What **materials** are needed to do the procedure

- The **steps** (**method**) for doing the procedure correctly

- How to **test** what is done to know that it is correct

1. Below are some parts of procedure texts. Underneath each one, write the part of the procedure (goal, materials, steps/method, test) to which it belongs. One has been done for you.

   Example:

   You will need a large sheet of paper and glue.

   materials _____

   a. After the bolts are tightened, the next step is to fit the cover over the battery.

   _____

   b. Follow these instructions for the best way to train your dog to fetch.

   _____

   c. The first step is to make sure that all the cables are plugged into the correct sockets.

   _____

   d. If the tail is the right weight, your kite should remain steady in the wind.

   _____

e. The following ingredients are needed: flour, sugar, butter, salt, baking powder, an egg, and some milk.

_____

f. Lastly, check your answer before going on to the next problem.

_____

g. The aim of this method of jumping is to increase the distance jumped.

_____

h. A screwdriver and a hammer are all the tools needed.

_____

i. If the model flies, you have been successful.

_____

j. Put the clamp on the edge of the wood and tighten the screws.

_____

k. If the puncture has been fixed correctly, no bubbles will show when the tube is put under water.

_____

l. Use this procedure to fix a squeaky hinge.

_____

m. Last of all, let the paint dry for 24 hours before using.

_____

n. As you tighten the bolt, you must take care not to damage the wooden top of the shelf.

_____

Name: _____

Writing Activity

Using what you've learned from this unit, write your own procedure. Be sure to include a goal, a list of materials, a list of steps (method), and testing results.

_____
_____
_____
_____
_____
_____
_____
_____
_____
_____
_____
_____
_____
_____
_____
_____
_____
_____
_____
_____
_____
_____
_____
_____
_____
_____

Paragraphs to Headings

Name: _____

The paragraphs A to E are out of order. Write the letter of each paragraph beside the heading to which it belongs in the chart below.

A The payload is all the equipment a satellite needs to do its job. This can include antennas, cameras, radar, and electronics. The payload is different for every satellite. For example, the payload for a weather satellite includes cameras to take pictures of cloud formations, while the payload for a communications satellite includes large antennas to transmit TV or telephone signals to Earth.

B A satellite is any object that orbits or revolves around another object. For example, the moon is a satellite of Earth, and Earth is a satellite of the sun.

C The bus is the part of the satellite that carries the payload and all its equipment into space. It holds all the satellite's parts together and provides electrical power, computers, and propulsion to the spacecraft. The bus also contains equipment that allows the satellite to communicate with Earth.

D Satellites come in many shapes and sizes and have many uses. Satellites are used to look at the weather, relay telephone and television signals, map Earth's surface, for navigation, and even for spying.

E A satellite is a complex machine. All satellites are made up of several subsystems that work together as one large system to help the satellite achieve its mission.

Headings	Paragraph
What Is a Satellite?	
Parts of a Satellite	
Uses of Satellites	
What Satellites Are Like	
What Satellites Carry into Space	

Name: _____

Reading Explanatory Text

Read this text on satellites. Pay attention to the details in order to complete the activities that follow.

Satellites

Relaying Messages

Many years ago, messages were sent over long distances using a relay system. For example, when the Romans won a battle in England, they lit a chain of fires. Each fire was a long way from the next. The light from the fire could be seen as soon as it was lit, even though it was a long way away. This is a relay system. Today, we use communication satellites far out in space to be the relay for messages. We use them to relay telephone calls, television images, and the Internet.

Communication satellites in a geosynchronous orbit (from geo = Earth + synchronous = moving at the same rate) are at a distance far enough out in space that, although they travel very fast, they always remain over one spot on Earth. Because they are so high up, they can see over large distances. The part of Earth that they can "see" is called the satellite's "footprint." For example, there is a satellite high above Australia that has a footprint that covers the whole continent. A person anywhere in Australia can use this satellite to communicate with anyone else in the country. These satellites can also communicate with other satellites out in space, so that a message may be sent in an instant around the whole world.

We use satellites as a relay system to send signals anywhere on Earth. If you wanted to send a signal from Australia to Italy, you could bounce, or relay, the signal using more than one satellite.

Satellites are not all the same. Communication satellites are high in the sky and stay over the same spot on Earth. These satellites circle close to Earth. They are in a low Earth orbit (LEO). Satellites in LEO are just 200–500 miles high. These LEO machines must travel very fast so that Earth's gravity won't pull them back into the atmosphere. Satellites in LEO speed along at more than 15,000 miles per hour. At this speed, they can complete an Earth orbit in about 90 minutes.

Satellites *(cont.)*

The Use of Low Earth Orbit

Because a low Earth orbit is near Earth, it gives a clearer view of the surface below. The space shuttle crews have taken many detailed and stunning pictures of Earth from a low Earth orbit. Satellites that are used to measure things on our planet, like remote sensing and weather satellites, travel in LEOs because, from this lower orbit, they can capture very detailed pictures of Earth's surface.

Space Junk

Space around Earth, especially in the LEO area, is full of space "junk" as well as operating satellites. The United States Space Command (USSC) keeps track of the number of satellites in orbit. They report that there are more than 8,000 objects larger than a softball now circling the globe.

There is so much junk out there that it is becoming a worry. Most of the things in LEO are not working satellites. There are pieces of old rockets, broken satellites, tools lost by astronauts, and garbage left by astronauts as they worked in space stations. At 15,000 miles/hour, even a small bolt can hit a space shuttle with the impact of a small bomb. This is why the US Space Command keeps track of all the space junk.

Words in Context

1. The following words have special meanings in the text. Write the special meaning of the word(s) on the lines.

   a. **relaying**

   _____

   _____

   b. **footprint**

   _____

   _____

   c. **low Earth orbit**

   _____

   _____

Name: _____

Words in Context (cont.)

d. **synchronous**

_____

_____

e. **images**

_____

_____

f. **remote sensing**

_____

_____

g. **space junk**

_____

_____

h. **surface**

_____

_____

i. **satellites**

_____

_____

j. **USSC**

_____

_____

k. **astronaut**

_____

_____

l. **geo**

_____

_____

Attending to Details

Name: _____

1. Complete the following sentences based on the texts in this unit.

   a. It is important to have a record of all the **space junk** because _____

   _____

   _____

   b. A **low Earth orbit** satellite has some advantages over geosynchronous

   orbits that allow it to _____

   _____

   _____

   c. The **bus** is the main part of a satellite because it _____

   _____

   _____

   d. All satellites are **complex machines** because they are made _____

   _____

   _____

   e. Although all satellites have many parts that are the same, the **payload** is

   different because it is _____

   _____

   _____

   f. The **footprint** of a satellite is the _____

   _____

   _____

   g. Satellites have many **uses** such as _____

   _____

   _____

Name: _____

Writing Activity

Why are satellites such complex machines? What other complex machines help you in your day-to-day life? Explain your answers.

_____
_____
_____
_____
_____
_____
_____
_____
_____
_____
_____
_____
_____
_____
_____
_____
_____
_____
_____
_____
_____
_____
_____
_____

62

Reading Reports

Name: _____

Read the following text, keeping this question in mind as you read:

> **How have these deep-sea creatures adapted to living so far underwater?**

Strange Creatures of the Deep Sea

The deepest parts of the seas are dark and cold. The pressure of the water is so great that it can crush people. Even with diving suits and air to breathe, men and women cannot go any deeper than 200 miles. Yet in this dark, cold world, there are sea animals that live and hunt in very deep places.

The animals that live in the deep sea have special ways of hunting and swimming around. Here are two examples:

The Dragonfish

The dragonfish is a deep-sea creature.

This fish grows to about 6 inches in length. It has a large head with big eyes and a large mouth. It has many sharp, fang-like teeth. The dragonfish has a long barbel, or stem of flesh, attached to its chin. This barbel is tipped with a light-making organ known as a photophore. The dragonfish also has photophores along the sides of its body.

Dragonfish live in deep ocean waters at depths of up to 1,000 miles. They are found in most tropical regions around the world.

The dragonfish uses its light-making organ (photophore) like a fishing lure, flashing it on and off and waving it back and forth. This light attracts other fish and draws them close. Once an unsuspecting fish gets too close, it is snapped up in the dragonfish's powerful jaws. The photophores along the sides of its body may be used to signal other dragonfish during mating. They may also serve to attract and disorient prey from deep below.

Name: _____

Reading Reports (cont.)

Strange Creatures of the Deep Sea (cont.)

The Gulper Eel

The gulper eel is one of the strangest creatures in the sea. It is a bony fish that belongs to the eel family of sea animals. It is sometimes called the pelican eel (*Eurypharynx pelecanoides*) or umbrella mouth gulper because of its mouth.

The gulper eel is perhaps one of the most bizarre-looking creatures in the deep ocean. It has a very large, unusual mouth. This eel's mouth is loosely hinged and can be opened wide enough to swallow an animal much larger than itself. The prey is then put into a pouch-like lower jaw, which is like that of a pelican. In fact, this animal is often referred to as the pelican eel for this reason. The gulper's stomach can also stretch to make room for its large meals. This giant mouth gives the eel its other common name of umbrella mouth gulper. The eel has a very long, whip-like tail. Specimens that have been brought to the surface in fishing nets have been known to have their long tails tied into several knots. The gulper eel grows to a length of about 20 to 70 inches.

The gulper eel is found in all of the world's oceans, in warm waters at depths ranging from 1,000 to 1,700 miles.

The gulper eel is a fast swimmer. This fish eats other fish, shrimp, and plankton (copepods). It gets its prey by acting like a living net, swimming onto the prey with a large, open mouth. Although it can eat prey that is larger than itself, it generally eats smaller sea animals.

Dictionary Meanings

1. Use a dictionary to help you write the definitions for the following words, which can be found in the text.

a. bizarre	
b. specimen	
c. organ	
d. lure	

64

Comparing and Contrasting

Name: _____

In the table below, compare and contrast the features of dragonfish and gulper eels. Use the art and facts from the text to help you.

Feature	Dragonfish	Gulper Eel
a. Length		
b. Number of light-making organs		
c. Shape of tail		
d. Depth where it hunts		
e. Main place where it lives		
f. Mouth		
g. Eyes		
h. Kind of teeth		

Name: _____

Planning a Report

Knowing how to write a report is a useful skill. Look at the fact boxes below. Each one will become a paragraph in a report on the orca. You may use all or only some of the facts in each box. To further help you write a report, review the steps below. Write your report on page 67.

Classification Facts

- orca or "killer whale"
- largest member of dolphin family of whales
- sea mammal

Description Facts

- large round body, up to 30 ft. long
- weighs up to 12,000 lbs.
- huge jaws with 40 to 52 strong teeth
- large dorsal fin
- mostly black on top and white underneath

Location Facts

- lives in pods of 6–40 whales
- found in all oceans
- seems to like colder waters

Dynamic Facts

- a fierce hunter
- eats all kinds of marine animals such as sharks, fish, squid, seals, penguins, and seagulls
- a fast swimmer
- will protect their young and other members of the pod who are sick or injured

Steps for Writing a Report

- Give your report a title.
- Collect facts about the animal or thing and organize them into the correct planning groups. (This has been done for you.)
- Turn your facts into sentences and then make a paragraph. You will have four paragraphs. (Each set of facts will be a separate paragraph.) Do not worry about overlap or repetition at this time.
- Edit your draft paragraphs. Review the dragonfish report as an example. Replace words you have repeated too often. Rewrite sentences or delete parts not needed.
- Read your work aloud to yourself to hear if it makes sense.
- Proofread your report for spelling and punctuation.
- Have a conference with a writing partner or the teacher to check what you have done.
- Write your final copy. Remember to leave a line between paragraphs.

Notes: **Possible beginnings for paragraphs**

Classification paragraph:

The orca is . . .

Description paragraph:

The orca has a . . .

Location paragraph:

The orca is found . . .

Dynamic paragraph.

The orca can . . .

Writing a Report

Name: _____

In the space below, write your orca report. Follow the steps on page 66. The title has been provided for you.

The Orca (Killer Whale)

_____

_____

_____

_____

_____

_____

_____

_____

_____

_____

_____

_____

_____

_____

_____

_____

_____

_____

_____

_____

_____

_____

_____

Name: _____

Reading for Information

Read the short texts about each of the prehistoric animals below in order to complete the activities that follow.

Giant Animals of Long Ago

Procoptodon goliah

This giant marsupial was the largest of the leaf-eating kangaroos and weighed about 450 lbs. It could stand on tiptoe, prop itself on its tail, and reach leaves up to 10 ft. from the ground. The skull was short and deep. With its powerful jaws, it could grind very tough leaves.

Palorchestes azael

This giant marsupial was once thought to be a giant kangaroo. As more fossils of this species were found, researchers realized that it must have walked on four legs. *Palorchestes* may also have had a small trunk, hence the name "marsupial tapir."

Thylacoleo carnifex

This large animal is called the marsupial lion. It weighed from 200 to 450 lbs. It had a cat-like skull with large, sharp slicing teeth. It also had a large retractable thumb claw and powerful front legs. This animal was a fearsome predator.

Diprotodon australis

This was the largest marsupial to ever live in Australia, weighing over 4,000 lbs. It was somewhat like a huge marsupial bear. Because of its size, it would have had few enemies.

Thylacinus cynocephalus

The thylacine or Tasmanian tiger is now extinct. The last one died in the Hobart Zoo in 1936. Each year, reports of sightings in remote spots are made, but there has been no proof presented to show the animal is still alive. The cat-like head and the stripes on its back are similar to those of a tiger. Its sharp teeth and claws were used for hunting smaller animals.

Giant Animals of Long Ago *(cont.)*

Megalibgwilia ramsayi

This monotreme was a very large, long-beaked echidna about the size of a sheep. It had powerful digging forelimbs. This animal's food would probably have included worms and grubs rather than ants.

Wonambi naracoortensis

Wonambi was a large, non-venomous snake that grew to a length of 15 to 20 ft. and killed its prey by constriction. "Wonambi" is an Aboriginal word for the rainbow serpent.

Megalania prisca

This reptile was a huge goanna. It was 20 ft. long and able to look a man in the eye. It had strong, sharp teeth and powerful claws.

Proving Understanding

1. Write a sentence or sentences below each statement to prove they are true. Use information from the text to help you.

   a. *Thylacoleo* was a fearsome predator.

   _____

   _____

   _____

   b. We have an accurate idea of how the Tasmanian tiger looked.

   _____

   _____

   _____

   c. *Diprotodon* probably had few enemies.

   _____

   _____

   _____

Name: _____

Proving Understanding (cont.)

d. *Palorchestes azael* was probably not a large kangaroo as once thought.

_____

_____

_____

e. *Megalania* was bigger than a goanna of today.

_____

_____

_____

f. *Wonambi* was known to human beings.

_____

_____

_____

g. *Megalibgwilia* would need to eat more than ants to survive.

_____

_____

_____

h. *Thylacinus* was similar to a tiger.

_____

_____

_____

i. *Diprotodon* was the largest Australian marsupial.

_____

_____

_____

j. *Procoptodon* could eat leaves from trees.

_____

_____

Comparing Information   Name: _____

1. Find the information in the text and record it in the correct box alongside each animal listed in the table below. If no information is given, write "NI" in the box.

Animal	Kind of Animal	Size	Food	Important Features
a. *Procoptodon goliah*				
b. *Palorchestes azael*				
c. *Thylacoleo carnifex*				
d. *Diprotodon australis*				
e. *Thylacinus cynocephalus*				
f. *Megalibgwilia ramsayi*				
g. *Wonambi naracoortensis*				
h. *Megalania prisca*				

Combining Sentences

1. Below and on the next page are groups of short sentences. Write one sentence that has the same meaning as the sentences in each group.

   a. *Megalania* was huge.
      Megalania was a goanna.

   _____

   _____

Name: _____

Combining Sentences (cont.)

b. *Wonambi* was not poisonous.
   Wonambi was a large snake.

   _____

   _____

c. The last thylacine died in 1936.
   It died in the Hobart Zoo.

   _____

   _____

d. *Thylacoleo* was a marsupial lion.
   This marsupial lion had a skull like a cat.
   This animal had large slicing teeth.

   _____

   _____

   _____

e. Once it was thought to be a kangaroo.
   Now *Palorchestes* is thought to be a marsupial tapir.
   It may have had a small trunk.

   _____

   _____

   _____

f. *Procoptodon* was the largest leaf-eating kangaroo.
   Procoptodon was a giant marsupial.
   It ate leaves in trees.

   _____

   _____

   _____

g. *Megalibgwilia* was a huge echidna.
   It was the size of a sheep.
   It had powerful digging forelimbs.

   _____

   _____

   _____

Missing Words

Name: _____

Show which words in the box alongside this text go in the spaces by writing the letter that represents each word.

1. The Tasmanian tiger is an interesting ☐. It is called the Tasmanian ☐ because of its striped coat and because it lived only in Tasmania in modern times. Up until 2,000 ☐ ago, the Tasmanian tiger could be found in open forests and woodlands across mainland ☐ and even in New Guinea.

    a. tiger
    b. Australia
    c. animal
    d. years

2. The Tasmanian tiger was a ☐ that hunted wallabies and other ☐, including sheep. Its closest living ☐ are numbats and other carnivorous marsupials, such as quolls and the Tasmanian ☐.

    a. mammals
    b. meat-eater
    c. Devil
    d. relatives

3. Fossils of the Tasmanian tiger have been ☐ in many places in Australia as well as in New ☐. These ☐ include complete carcasses and a mummified thylacine from a cave on the Nullarbor ☐.

    a. found
    b. fossils
    c. Guinea
    d. Plain

4. The thylacine became ☐ in 1936—the same year it was declared a protected species. It may have died out on ☐ Australia because of competition with the dingo. The ☐ does not live in ☐, which was the home of the Tasmanian tiger until Europeans arrived and ☐ it to extinction.

    a. dingo
    b. hunted
    c. extinct
    d. Tasmania
    e. mainland

Name: _____

Logical Order

1. Each sequence on the left has four parts, with the last part unfinished. On the right are 3 parts: A, B, and C, one of which fits the sequence. Write the letter that represents part 4 in the box.

a.   [ ]

  1　　2　　3　　4　　　A　　B　　C

b.   [ ]

  1　　2　　3　　4　　　A　　B　　C

c.

  1　　2　　3　　4　　　A　　B　　C

d. (triangles with dots)

  1　　2　　3　　4　　　A　　B　　C

e.

  1　　2　　3　　4　　　A　　B　　C

f. | made | make | mane | [ ] | | more | mate | mite |

  1　　2　　3　　4　　　A　　B　　C

g. | ac | df | gi | [ ] | | jl | km | hj |

  1　　2　　3　　4　　　A　　B　　C

h.   brine [ ] brute booth broth

  1　　2　　3　　4　　　A　　B　　C

Answer Key

Unit 1

Paragraph Order   (page 5)

A–5   C–6   E–4   G–7
B–3   D–2   F–1

Understanding Details   (page 6)

1.

Statement	T	F	NE	PAR LETT
a. A worker bee brought Zeus the honey.		✗		B
b. Zeus could not go back on his promise because he was a god.	✗			A
c. Zeus liked honey more than any other food.			✗	
d. The queen bee was angry because men stole honey from the beehives.			✗	
e. The queen bee wanted to sting other bees.		✗		E
f. Zeus was entertained by people's adventures.	✗			A
g. The other gods told Zeus to be kind to women.			✗	
h. Zeus gave the queen bee her wish.	✗			C
i. Zeus did not like men and women because they had wars.		✗		A
j. The animals, as well as men and women, went to Zeus for help because he was in the heavens and could see all things.			✗	
k. The bees were cunning and gave Zeus a present before asking for help.	✗			B
l. The bees did not have stingers before the queen bee went to Zeus.	✗			F
m. This story is a true account of how bees got stingers.		✗		F
n. The story was told in Greece over 2,500 years ago.	✗			F
o. Zeus let the bees sting but made it so they would die when they did because he did not like bees.			✗	

Words in Context   (page 7)

1. a. entertained
   b. promise
   c. adventures
   d. wish
   e. solving
   f. meekly
   g. wise
   h. Zeus

2. a. sad
   b. meekly
   c. old
   d. stop
   e. keep
   f. careful
   g. entertained
   h. dies

Sentencing Combining   (page 8)

1. Answers will vary.

Understanding Text   (page 9)

1. a. The queen bee lays a single egg in each cell.
   b. Each egg hatches into a larva.
   c. The cell is capped with wax, and the larva transforms into the pupa.
   d. A new adult worker bee emerges.

Unit 2

Writing a Recount   (pages 11–14)

1. Answers will vary.

Recognizing Time Markers   (page 16)

1. a. Long ago
   b. none
   c. When
   d. Before
   e. While
   f. none
   g. As
   h. none
   i. Once upon a time
   j. then
   k. Yesterday
   l. When
   m. then
   n. Long ago
   o. Soon
   p. After
   q. Until

Unit 3

Caption Matching   (page 18)

1. a. 3   d. 1   g. 1, 2, 3
   b. 1   e. 3   h. 1
   c. 1, 2   f. 1, 2   i. 3

Sentence Combining and Comprehension   (page 19)

Answers will vary.

True, False, or Can't Tell   (page 20)

1. a. CT   d. T   g. CT   j. CT
   b. T   e. F   h. CT   k. F
   c. T   f. CT   i. T

Understanding a Text   (page 21)

1. a. vehicles   d. mechanics
   b. fans   e. engines
   c. drivers   f. crashes

Puzzle Reasoning   (page 21)

1. a. 1st—white convertible
      2nd—red sedan
      3rd—blue truck
      4th—green SUV
   b. 1st—black coupe
      2nd—red convertible
      3rd—green sedan
      4th—orange truck
      5th—white SUV
      6th—blue van

Unit 4

Paragraph Order   (page 22)

A—2   B—1   C—6   D—4   E—5   F—3

Finding Evidence   (page 23)

1. Answers will vary.
2. Answers will vary. Sample answer: You cannot be trusted if you take both sides of an issue.

Same and Different   (page 24)

1. a. same   f. same
   b. different   g. same
   c. different   h. same
   d. same   i. different
   e. same   j. different

ANSWER KEY

Unit 4 (cont.)

Report Text Structure (page 25)
1. a. type of writing that presents information in a scientific way
   b. states what something is
   c. states what something has or looks like
   d. states where something lives and can be found
   e. states what something does and how it acts

Meaning Grid (Reports) (page 26)
1. a. classification
   b. description
   c. dynamics
   d. location
   e. classification
   f. description
   g. dynamics
   h. classification
   i. location
   j. description
   k. dynamics
   l. description
   m. classification
   n. dynamics
   o. dynamics
   p. location
   q. location
   r. classification

Unit 5

Paragraph Order (page 27)
A—6   B—8   C—4   D—5   E—7

Fact or Opinion (page 28)
1. a. fact   d. opinion   g. opinion
   b. opinion   e. fact   h. opinion
   c. fact   f. fact   i. opinion

Comparing and Contrasting (pages 30–31)
1. a. *Brachiosaurus, Triceratops, Ankylosaurus, Stegosaurus*
   b. They were not alive at the same time.
   c. *Brachiosaurus, Tyrannosaurus, Allosaurus, Stegosaurus, Carcharodontosaurus, Triceratops, Ankylosaurus*
   d. *Triceratops, Ankylosaurus*
   e. They had no enemies that preyed on them. Heavy plates would make it difficult for them to hunt.
   f. by swinging its huge, heavy tail
   g. *Brachiosaurus, Carcharodontosaurus, Tyrannosaurus, Allosaurus, Ankylosaurus, Stegosaurus, Triceratops*
   h. rhinoceros
   i. *Tyrannosaurus* was bigger and heavier than *Allosaurus*; they lived at different times; *Tyrannosaurus* had larger teeth.
   j. Late Jurassic: 156–140 million years ago; Middle Cretaceous: 110–90 million years ago; Late Cretaceous: 70–65 million years ago

Unit 6

Organizing Facts (pages 33–34)
1. Saltwater Crocodile is—crocodile; reptile; animal
   Saltwater Crocodile has—big, round body; four short, thick legs; sharp claws; strong, sharp teeth; long tail; large jaws; big head; small eyes

Saltwater Crocodile's location—warm tropical seas; on banks or shores
Saltwater Crocodile's dynamics—swims well; hunts other animals
2. Answers will vary.

Unit 7

Event Order (page 39)
1. a. 9   f. 2   k. 11
   b. 3   g. 4   l. 1
   c. 12   h. 7   m. 6
   d. 14   i. 10   n. 13
   e. 15   j. 8   o. 5

Evaluating Details (pages 40–41)
1. a. 1st, 2nd, 3rd   d. 2nd, 3rd, 4th
   b. 2nd, 3rd, 4th   e. 1st, 3rd, 4th
   c. 1st, 2nd   f. 3rd

Unit 8

Paragraph Order (page 44)
A—2   B—4   C—5   D—3   E—1

Wrong to Right (pages 44–45)
1. a. There was a farmer who had four big, strong sons.
   b. The farmer's sons were lazy and did not like to work.
   c. The farmer had an idea, so he called his sons together.
   d. The farmer told his sons, "There is treasure hidden on the farm. You will find it buried in the fields."
   e. The sons liked money, so they dug up the fields. One son dug up the east field, another the west field. The third son dug up the south field, and the fourth son dug up the north field.

Choose the Sentence Ending (page 46)
1. a. 3rd   c. 4th
   b. 4th   d. 4th

Fact or Opinion (page 47)
1. Answers will vary. Possible answers:
   a. fact, D   g. opinion, C
   b. fact, D   h. opinion
   c. opinion, E   i. opinion, D
   d. opinion, D   j. fact, B
   e. opinion   k. opinion
   f. opinion   l. opinion

Combining Sentences (page 48)
1. Answers will vary.

Picture Interpretation (pages 49–50)
1. a. PT   d. F   g. PT   j. PT
   b. F   e. F   h. PT   k. PF
   c. PT   f. PT   i. F   l. T

Answer Key *(cont.)*

Unit 9

Drawing Conclusions   (pages 52–53)

1. a. It needs to hold on to the balloon.
   b. The straw is smooth and straight.
   c. There is more air at a greater pressure.
   d. A tight string gives the straw a straight run with less drag.
   e. The smaller straw reduces the contact with the string. The contact slows the straw as it slides along.
   f. Possible answer: Aerosol cans contain air that escapes under pressure.

Identifying Procedure Texts   (pages 54–55)

1. a. steps/method   h. materials
   b. goal   i. test
   c. steps/method   j. steps/method
   d. test   k. test
   e. materials   l. goal
   f. test   m. steps/method
   g. goal   n. steps/method

Unit 10

Paragraphs to Headings   (page 57)

B
C
D
E
A

Words in Context   (pages 59–60)

1. a. passing on
   b. the area of Earth covered by a satellite's sensors
   c. an orbit 200–500 miles high
   d. the same or together
   e. pictures or patterns
   f. measuring from a long distance away
   g. bits and pieces of old satellites and tools
   h. ground below
   i. objects that revolve around other objects
   j. United States Space Command
   k. space traveler
   l. Earth

Attending to Details   (page 61)

1. a. space junk can damage other satellites.
   b. see a surface in greater detail.
   c. is the base on which all other parts are joined.
   d. up of several subsystems that work together as one large system.
   e. all the equipment a satellite needs to do a particular job.
   f. area of Earth's surface that the satellite covers or senses.
   g. telephone and TV communications, mapping, navigation, photographs, weather, and space exploration.

Unit 11

Dictionary Meanings   (page 64)

1. a. weird, strange, and unusual
   b. example of a thing, or something being scientifically studied
   c. a part of the body that has a specific function
   d. attract, entice, bring closer

Comparing and Contrasting   (page 65)

1. Answers will vary. Sample answers:
   a. 6 inches/20–70 inches
   b. many photophores/unknown
   c. flat and uneven/very long and whip-like
   d. up to 1,000 miles/1,000–1,700 miles
   e. tropical regions/all oceans—warmer waters
   f. large mouth/very large, loosely hinged mouth
   g. big eyes/small eyes near the tip of its top jaw
   h. many sharp, fang-like teeth/many long and thin teeth

Unit 12

Proving Understanding   (pages 69–70)

1. Answers will vary.

Comparing Information   (page 71)

1.

	Animal	Kind of Animal	Size	Food	Important Features
a.	*Procoptodon goliah*	kangaroo	giant—weighed up to 450 lbs.	leaves on trees	short skull and powerful jaws
b.	*Palorchestes azael*	marsupial tapir	giant	NI	had a small trunk
c.	*Thylacoleo carnifex*	marsupial lion	large—weighed up to 450 lbs.	NI	sharp slicing teeth and retractable thumb claw
d.	*Diprotodon australis*	marsupial	weighed over 4,000 lbs.	NI	size of a large bear
e.	*Thylacinus cynocephalus*	Tasmanian tiger	NI	smaller animals	cat-like head and stripes
f.	*Megalibgwilia ramsayi*	echidna	size of a sheep	worms and grubs	long beak and powerful forelimbs
g.	*Wonambi naracoortensis*	snake	15 to 20 feet	NI	non-poisonous and constricts prey
h.	*Megalania prisca*	goanna	up to 20 feet long	NI	sharp teeth and powerful claws

Combining Sentences   (pages 71–72)

1. Answers will vary.

Missing Words   (page 73)

1. c, a, d, b   3. a, c, b, d
2. b, a, d, c   4. c, e, a, d, b

Logical Order   (page 74)

1. a. A   d. C   g. A
   b. C   e. B   h. C
   c. C   f. B

Meeting Standards

Each activity meets one or more of the following Common Core State Standards (© Copyright 2010. National Governors Association Center for Best Practices and Council of Chief State School Officers. All rights reserved.). For more information about the Common Core State Standards, go to *http://www.corestandards.org/* or *http://www.teachercreated.com/standards*.

Reading: Literature	Activity	Page
Key Ideas and Details		
ELA.RL.5.1: Quote accurately from a text when explaining what the text says explicitly and when drawing inferences from the text.	Unit 1—Understanding Details Unit 4—Finding Evidence Unit 8—Combining Sentences	6 23 48
ELA.RL.5.2: Determine a theme of a story, drama, or poem from details in the text, including how characters in a story or drama respond to challenges or how the speaker in a poem reflects upon a topic; summarize the text.	Unit 1—Paragraph Order Unit 4—Paragraph Order Unit 4—Finding Evidence Unit 8—Paragraph Order Unit 8—Choose the Sentence Ending	5 22 23 44 46
ELA.RL.5.3: Compare and contrast two or more characters, settings, or events in a story or drama, drawing on specific details in the text (e.g., how characters interact).	Unit 1—Understanding Details Unit 4—Paragraph Order Unit 4—Finding Evidence Unit 8—Fact or Opinion	6 22 23 47
Craft and Structure		
ELA.RL.5.4: Determine the meaning of words and phrases as they are used in a text, including figurative language such as metaphors and similes.	Unit 1—Words in Context Unit 7—Imaginative Report Unit 8—Paragraph Order Unit 8—Choose the Sentence Ending	7 42 44 46
ELA.RL.5.5: Explain how a series of chapters, scenes, or stanzas fits together to provide the overall structure of a particular story, drama, or poem.	Unit 1—Paragraph Order Unit 4—Paragraph Order Unit 7—Imaginative Report Unit 8—Paragraph Order	5 22 42 44
Range of Reading and Level of Text Complexity		
ELA.RL.5.10: By the end of the year, read and comprehend literature, including stories, dramas, and poetry, at the high end of the grades 4–5 text complexity band independently and proficiently.	Unit 1—Paragraph Order Unit 4—Paragraph Order Unit 4—Same and Different Unit 7—Imaginative Report Unit 8—Paragraph Order	5 22 24 42 44

Reading: Informational Text	Activity	Page	Activity	Page
Key Ideas and Details				
ELA.RI. 5.1: Quote accurately from a text when explaining what the text says explicitly and when drawing inferences from the text.	Unit 1—Understanding Text Unit 3—Caption Matching Unit 5—Paragraph Order Unit 5—Fact or Opinion Unit 5—Finding Facts	9 18 27 28 29	Unit 5—Comparing and Contrasting Unit 7—Evaluating Details Unit 10—Attending to Details Unit 12—Reading for Information Unit 12—Proving Understanding	30–31 40–41 61 68–69 69–70
ELA.RI.5.2: Determine two or more main ideas of a text and explain how they are supported by key details; summarize the text.	Unit 4—Report Text Structure Unit 7—Event Order Unit 10—Paragraphs to Headings	25 39 57	Unit 12—Reading for Information Unit 12—Proving Understanding	68–69 69–70
ELA.RI.5.3: Explain the relationships or interactions between two or more individuals, events, ideas, or concepts in a historical, scientific, or technical text based on specific information in the text.	Unit 3—Caption Matching Unit 4—Meaning Grid (Reports) Unit 5—Fact or Opinion Unit 5—Finding Facts Unit 5—Comparing and Contrasting Unit 9—Reading Procedures Unit 9—Drawing Conclusions	18 26 28 29 30–31 51–52 52–53	Unit 9—Identifying Procedure Texts Unit 11—Reading Reports Unit 11—Comparing and Contrasting Unit 12—Reading for Information Unit 12—Proving Understanding Unit 12—Comparing Information Unit 12—Logical Order	54–55 63–64 65 68–69 69–70 71 74
Craft and Structure				
ELA.RI.5.4: Determine the meaning of general academic and domain-specific words and phrases in a text relevant to a *grade 5 topic or subject area.*	*all activities*			
ELA.RI.5.5: Compare and contrast the overall structure (e.g., chronology, comparison, cause/effect, problem/solution) of events, ideas, concepts, or information in two or more texts.	Unit 5—Finding Facts Unit 5—Comparing and Contrasting Unit 9—Reading Procedures Unit 9—Drawing Conclusions Unit 11—Comparing and Contrasting	29 30–31 51–52 52–53 65		

78

Reading: Informational Text (cont.)	Activity	Page	Activity	Page
Integration of Knowledge and Ideas				
ELA.RI.5.7: Draw on information from multiple print or digital sources, demonstrating the ability to locate an answer to a question quickly or to solve a problem efficiently.	Unit 6—Organizing Facts Unit 10—Attending to Details	33–34 61		
Range of Reading and Level of Text Complexity				
ELA.RI.5.10: By the end of the year, read and comprehend informational texts, including history/social studies, science, and technical texts, at the high end of the grades 4–5 text complexity band independently and proficiently.	Unit 1—Understanding Text Unit 2—Reading Recounts Unit 2—Writing a Recount Unit 2—Understanding Time Words Unit 2—Recognizing Time Markers Unit 3—Reading About Racing Unit 3—Caption Matching Unit 3—Sentence Combining and Comprehension Unit 3—True, False, or Can't Tell Unit 3—Understanding a Text Unit 3—Puzzle Reasoning Unit 4—Report Text Structure Unit 4—Meaning Grid (Reports) Unit 5—Paragraph Order Unit 5—Fact or Opinion	9 10 11 15 16 17 18 19 20 21 21 25 26 27 28	Unit 5—Finding Facts Unit 6—Graphic Organizer Unit 6—Organizing Facts Unit 6—About Reports Unit 7—Reading for Information Unit 7—Event Order Unit 8—Picture Interpretation Unit 9—Reading Procedures Unit 9—Drawing Conclusions Unit 9—Identifying Procedure Texts Unit 10—Paragraphs to Headings Unit 10—Reading Explanatory Text Unit 11—Reading Reports Unit 11—Planning a Report Unit 12—Reading for Information Unit 12—Missing Words	29 32 33–34 35 37–38 39 49–50 51–52 52–53 54–55 57 58–59 63–64 66 68–69 73

Writing	Activity	Page	Activity	Page
Text Types and Purposes				
ELA.W.5.2: Write informative/ explanatory texts to examine a topic and convey ideas and information clearly.	Unit 6—Organizing Facts Unit 6—About Reports Unit 6—Writing a Report Unit 9—Drawing Conclusions	33–34 35 36 52–53	Unit 9—Writing Activity Unit 10—Writing Activity Unit 11—Writing a Report Unit 12—Combining Sentences	56 62 67 71–72
ELA.W.5.3: Write narratives to develop real or imagined experiences or events using effective technique, descriptive details, and clear event sequences.	Unit 2—Writing a Recount Unit 7—Writing an Imaginative Report Unit 10—Writing Activity	11–14 43 62		
Production and Distribution of Writing				
ELA.W.5.4: Produce clear and coherent writing in which the development and organization are appropriate to task, purpose, and audience. (Grade-specific expectations for writing types are defined in standards 1–3 above.)	Unit 1—Sentence Combining Unit 2—Writing a Recount Unit 3—Sentence Combining and Comprehension Unit 5—Comparing and Contrasting Unit 6—Writing a Report Unit 7—Writing an Imaginative Report Unit 8—Wrong to Right	8 11–12 19 30–31 36 43 44–45	Unit 9—Drawing Conclusions Unit 9—Writing Activity Unit 10—Attending to Details Unit 10—Writing Activity Unit 11—Writing a Report Unit 12—Reading for Information Unit 12—Combining Sentences	52–53 56 61 62 67 68–69 71–72
ELA.W.5.5: With guidance and support from peers and adults, develop and strengthen writing as needed by planning, revising, editing, rewriting, or trying a new approach.	Unit 2—Writing a Recount	11–14		
Range of Writing				
ELA.W.5.10: Write routinely over extended time frames (time for research, reflection, and revision) and shorter time frames (a single sitting or a day or two) for a range of discipline-specific tasks, purposes, and audiences.	Unit 1—Sentence Combining Unit 2—Writing a Recount Unit 3—Sentence Combining and Comprehension Unit 4—Finding Evidence Unit 4—Report Text Structure Unit 5—Comparing and Contrasting Unit 6—Organizing Facts Unit 6—Writing a Report Unit 7—Writing an Imaginative Report Unit 8—Wrong to Right	8 11–14 19 23 25 30–31 34 36 43 44–45	Unit 8—Combining Sentences Unit 9—Drawing Conclusions Unit 9—Identifying Procedure Texts Unit 9—Writing Activity Unit 10—Words in Context Unit 10—Attending to Details Unit 10—Writing Activity Unit 11—Comparing and Contrasting Unit 11—Planning a Report Unit 12—Proving Understanding Unit 12—Combining Sentences	48 52–53 54–55 56 59–60 61 62 65 66 69–70 71–72

UNION COUNTY PUBLIC LIBRARY
316 E. Windsor St., Monroe, NC 28112

Meeting Standards (cont.)

MEETING STANDARDS

Language	Activity	Page	Activity	Page
Conventions of Standard English				
ELA.L.5.1: Demonstrate command of the conventions of standard English grammar and usage when writing or speaking.	Unit 1—Sentence Combining	8	Unit 8—Combining Sentences	48
	Unit 2—Writing a Recount	11–14	Unit 9—Drawing Conclusions	52–53
	Unit 3—Sentence Combining and Comprehension	19	Unit 9—Writing Activity	56
			Unit 10—Attending to Details	61
	Unit 5—Finding Facts	29	Unit 10—Writing Activity	62
	Unit 5—Comparing and Contrasting	30–31	Unit 11—Writing a Report	67
	Unit 6—Writing a Report	36	Unit 12—Reading for Information	68–69
	Unit 7—Writing an Imaginative Report	43	Unit 12—Combining Sentences	71–72
	Unit 8—Wrong to Right	44–45		
ELA.L.5.2: Demonstrate command of the conventions of standard English capitalization, punctuation, and spelling when writing.	Unit 1—Sentence Combining	8	Unit 8—Wrong to Right	44–45
	Unit 2—Writing a Recount	11–14	Unit 8—Combining Sentences	48
	Unit 3—Sentence Combining and Comprehension	19	Unit 9—Drawing Conclusions	52–53
			Unit 9—Writing Activity	56
	Unit 4—Finding Evidence	23	Unit 10—Attending to Details	61
	Unit 5—Finding Facts	29	Unit 10—Writing Activity	62
	Unit 5—Comparing and Contrasting	30–31	Unit 11—Writing a Report	67
	Unit 6—Organizing Facts	34	Unit 12—Reading for Information	68–69
	Unit 6—Writing a Report	36	Unit 12—Comparing Information	71
	Unit 7—Writing an Imaginative Report	43	Unit 12—Combining Sentences	71–72
Knowledge of Language				
ELA.L.5.3: Use knowledge of language and its conventions when writing, speaking, reading, or listening.	Unit 1—Sentence Combining	8	Unit 7—Writing an Imaginative Report	43
	Unit 1—Writing a Recount	12–14	Unit 8—Wrong to Right	44–45
	Unit 3—Sentence Combining and Comprehension	19	Unit 8—Combining Sentences	48
			Unit 9—Drawing Conclusions	52–53
	Unit 3—Understanding a Text	21	Unit 9—Writing Activity	56
	Unit 3—Puzzle Reasoning	21	Unit 10—Attending to Details	61
	Unit 4—Finding Evidence	23	Unit 10—Writing Activity	62
	Unit 4—Meaning Grid (Reports)	26	Unit 11—Writing a Report	67
	Unit 5—Finding Facts	29	Unit 12—Reading for Information	68–69
	Unit 5—Comparing and Contrasting	30–31	Unit 12—Combining Sentences	71–72
	Unit 6—Writing a Report	36		
Vocabulary Acquisition and Use				
ELA.L.5.4: Determine or clarify the meaning of unknown and multiple-meaning words and phrases based on grade 5 reading and content, choosing flexibly from a range of strategies.	all activities			
ELA.L.5.5: Demonstrate understanding of figurative language, word relationships, and nuances in word meanings.	Unit 1—Words in Context	7	Unit 8—Combining Sentences	48
	Unit 2—Understanding Time Words	15	Unit 10—Words in Context	59–60
	Unit 2—Recognizing Time Markers	16	Unit 10—Attending to Details	61
	Unit 3—Understanding a Text	21	Unit 11—Dictionary Meanings	64
	Unit 4—Same and Different	24	Unit 12—Proving Understanding	69–70
	Unit 8—Wrong to Right	44–45	Unit 12—Missing Words	73
ELA.L.5.6: Acquire and use accurately grade-appropriate general academic and domain-specific words and phrases, including those that signal contrast, addition, and other logical relationships (e.g., *however, although, nevertheless, similarly, moreover, in addition*).	Unit 1—Words in Context	7	Unit 7—Evaluating Details	40–41
	Unit 1—Sentence Combining	8	Unit 7—Imaginative Report	42
	Unit 2—Writing a Recount	11–14	Unit 7—Writing an Imaginative Report	43
	Unit 2—Understanding Time Words	15	Unit 8—Paragraph Order	44
	Unit 2—Recognizing Time Markers	16	Unit 8—Wrong to Right	44–45
	Unit 3—Sentence Combining and Comprehension	19	Unit 8—Combining Sentences	48
			Unit 8—Picture Interpretation	49–50
	Unit 3—True, False, or Can't Tell	20	Unit 9—Reading Procedures	51–52
	Unit 3—Understanding a Text	21	Unit 9—Drawing Conclusions	52–53
	Unit 3—Puzzle Reasoning	21	Unit 9—Identifying Procedure Texts	54–55
	Unit 4—Same and Different	24	Unit 9—Writing Activity	56
	Unit 4—Meaning Grid (Reports)	26	Unit 10—Words in Context	59–60
	Unit 5—Paragraph Order	27	Unit 10—Attending to Details	61
	Unit 5—Finding Facts	29	Unit 11—Dictionary Meanings	64
	Unit 5—Comparing and Contrasting	30–31	Unit 11—Planning a Report	66–67
	Unit 6—Graphic Organizer	32	Unit 12—Proving Understanding	69–70
	Unit 6—Organizing Facts	33–34	Unit 12—Combining Sentences	71–72
	Unit 6—About Reports	35	Unit 12—Missing Words	73
	Unit 6—Writing a Report	36		